NORTH EAST TRACTION

NORTH EAST TRACTION

TRACTION

John Dedman

AMBERLEY

Front Cover: In bright morning sunshine DB red 60010 is passing the semaphores at Barnetby with the 6K21 08:11 Santon to Immingham empty iron ore tippler wagons. In the Railfreight Sectorisation era of the early 1990s, 60010 was in Construction Sector livery and had the name *Pumlumon Plynlimon*, which is a peak in the Cambrian Mountains. 19 October 2015.

Rear Cover: GBRF 66720 in what is known as the rainbow livery at Burton Salmon with the 6C96 10:34 Tyne Coal Terminal to Eggborough Power Station coal hoppers. GBRF held a competition for the children of its employees to design a loco livery and this was the winning entry by Emily Goodman. The other side of the loco has a different livery with similar colours. 9 October 2013

First published 2017

Amberley Publishing
The Hill, Stroud
Gloucestershire, GL5 4EP

www.amberley-books.com

Copyright © John Dedman, 2017

The right of John Dedman to be identified as the Author of this work has been asserted in accordance with the Copyrights, Designs and Patents Act 1988.

ISBN 978 1 4456 6634 1 (print)
ISBN 978 1 4456 6635 8 (ebook)

British Library Cataloguing in Publication Data.
A catalogue record for this book is available from the British Library.

Origination by Amberley Publishing.
Printed in the UK.

Introduction

My first visit to the North East of England was in 1980, not specifically for railway photography, but as always I was equipped for the odd occasions when I could go lineside for an hour or two. I was pleased to see how different it was from my local area on the South Coast, with the variety of locos and types of freight.

This first visit encouraged me to make more trips north – my most recent being in 2015. The areas covered in this volume are Humberside, Teesside, and Tyneside on the coast and inland Doncaster to Leeds, Darlington, and Newcastle. Some of the areas covered are very industrial, which produces some of the heaviest freight flows in the country, including steel, coal, and petroleum products.

My main targets were freight services but also included are passenger workings as well as visits to some of the loco depots in the area. Included are two visits to Thornaby Depot in 1988 which had a large allocation of various loco classes many in individual liveries with the kingfisher depot logo. Included were the Class 20s, refurbished Class 37/5s, and Class 47s, all of which had members with one off or modified liveries.

In the early 1980s my visits found locos of classes 25, 31, 37, 40, 45, and 47 quite common, by the end of the decade the Class 25 and 40 had gone and freights were in the hands of classes 20, 31, 37, 47, and 56. In the early 1990s the Class 60s were introduced and they took over many of the long distance heavy freight workings; these included oil trains previously worked by pairs of Class 31s and steel trains which were previously worked by pairs of Class 37s. They were also replacing pairs of Class 37s on the Scunthorpe iron ore trips from Immingham. Some of these double headed workings are included in this volume. By the late 1990s privatisation had taken over and the Class 66s were introduced. Many of the traditional locos had been retired, but as can be seen there was still work for some members of classes 37, 47, 56, and 60 in the area, and in the last few years the scene is dominated by Class 66 locos from GBRF, Freightliner, and DBS, with a handful of Class 60s still working heavy oil trains. As the variety of loco classes has diminished over the years, so the amount of liveries has increased – a good example being the GBRF Class 66s with some of their various liveries shown.

As with most parts of the country, the majority of passenger trains are now handled by multiple units of various types, of which some are included. The East Coast Main Line services are mostly powered by Class 91 locos with High Speed Trains sets still soldiering on mainly on through services to Scottish cities north of Edinburgh.

I have included some photos from friends who have visited the area, which fill some gaps in my collection as they have visited different locations and in different time periods, giving the book more variety of locations, loco liveries, and services.

The photos are arranged roughly into date order, starting with my first visit in 1980, which means some of the locations are visited more than once over the years.

I would like to acknowledge and thank the following people for their help and the information they have supplied: James Skoyles, Porcy Mane, and David Hayes.

I am also very grateful to the following who have allowed me to use their photos: Pete Nurse, Mark Bulger, John Fox, Mark Jamieson, Gordon White, Mark Finch, Steve Clark, Simon Lindsell, Andy Picton, and Ray Kingswell.

25288 is heading south on the East Coast Main Line with a mixed freight of vacuum braked wagons with a brake van bringing up the rear. South Otterington, 9 June 1980.

Headcode disc fitted 40007 is heading north at South Otterington with a selection of loaded steel wagons on 9 June 1980.

Heading south on the East Coast Main Line with a load of two dozen 45-ton fuel oil tanks are a pair of rail blue Class 31s – 31201 and 31282. South Otterington, 9 June 1980.

Class 45 Peak No. 45013 at South Otterington with a southbound Speedlink on 9 June 1980. Behind the loco are twelve white-roofed VDA vans with an empty car-carrying set behind the first van. The vans may well have originated from Rowntree's at Coxlodge (Fawdon), which was served by the freight-only branch to ICI Callerton, North Tyneside (now part of the Tyne & Wear Metro).

BR Blue 31274 is heading an Up mixed freight at South Otterington on 9 June 1980. Among the consignment are an Engineers wagon and coach, and revenue wagons with steel loads.

40074 is heading north at South Otterington with a Parcels train on 9 June 1980. It is made up of four BR bogie GUV vans with a BR BG full brake on the rear.

Two Class 108 diesel multiple units in white livery with a blue stripe are forming the 17:16 York to Darlington. Some units were turned out in this attractive livery when refurbished during the late 1970s. South Otterington, 9 June 1980.

An unidentified Class 47 is heading north on the East Coast Main Line at Ferryhill Gap with seven VDA vans. The vans have white roofs, which indicates they are probably heading for Rowntrees at Fawdon via Tyne Yard. The line climbing to West Cornforth and East Hetton Colliery can be seen in the background. 12 June 1980.

25189 is heading south at Ferryhill on the East Coast Main Line with 6M79 16:55 Gateshead TCFD to Bescot Speedlink on 12 June 1980. Behind the loco is a Cartic 4 with some Rowntrees white-roofed VDA vans at the rear.

Class 40 40011 has charge of a northbound Parcels service near Ferryhill on the East Coast Main Line. The vans include four ex-Southern Railway Utility vans, a BR BG full brake, three BR bogie GUV vans, and two BR CCT vans. 12 June 1980.

40083 is on the East Coast Main Line near Ferryhill with a mixed freight on 12 June 1980. Location is Coxhoe Junction looking towards Metal Bridge, which was the site of Rosedale and Ferryhill Ironworks. There was a complex set of lines and junctions here at one time.

An unidentified Class 46 is southbound at York with a mix of coaches and vans on 19 November 1981. The train is made up of mainly blue/grey liveried BGs with an ex-works second class Mk 1 behind the loco. Further back is a plain blue BG, a Mk 2 Brake First, and a couple of blue GUVs.

Three unidentified locos of classes 47, 40, and 46, all in BR standard blue livery, are at York on 19 November 1981.

Deltic 55002 *The King's Own Yorkshire Light Infantry* was repainted into its original BR green livery in 1980 and is seen here running light engine at York on 19 November 1981. It is now preserved and based at the National Railway Museum at York.

37080 is heading south through Doncaster station with a long set of HTV coal hoppers on 19 November 1981. In the Railfreight Sectorisation era of the late 1980s, 37080 was repainted in the Petroleum Sector livery. It was withdrawn from service in 1996 and cut up the following year.

E52105 is leading a four-car Class 123 unit at Doncaster on 19 November 1981. Ten of these units were built at Swindon in the early 1960s and used on various services on the Western Region until the late 1970s when they were transferred to the Eastern Region. Here they were used on Trans Pennine services from Hull to Manchester and Sheffield. The sets were all withdrawn by 1984 and none were preserved.

55015 and 31264 at the head of a line of withdrawn locos at Doncaster Works in 1981. 55015 has the Finsbury Park white cab windows but has lost its *Tulyar* nameplates. Behind 31264 are another six withdrawn Deltics. (Ray Kingswell)

An unidentified Class 40 at Scarborough with a fine array of signals on the gantry. The Class 08 is about to remove stock from an arrival at the platform. (Ray Kingswell)

03066 is engaged with carriage shunting duties at Newcastle on 3 April 1985. The loco has a short wheelbase so it is coupled to a shunters wagon to ensure operation of track circuits, which would not always detect such a short wheelbase loco when running solo. The cylinder mounted in front of the cab is for the air brakes, which have been added to this loco. (Mark Jamieson)

45069 and 31260 are stabled at Frodingham Depot on 8 June 1986. (Pete Nurse)

47578 *The Royal Society of Edinburgh* stands at Leeds station waiting to depart with a Trans Pennine passenger train. The loco is in large logo blue livery with the Eastfield Depot Scottie dog below the nameplate. In 1991 this loco was repainted in Rail Express Systems livery and renamed *Respected*; in 1994 it was converted to Class 47/7 and renumbered 47776. (Pete Nurse)

Under the magnificence of York station stands 47656, which had arrived on 1E30 09:24 Bristol Temple Meads to York; having run-round the locomotive waits time before heading back south with 1V60 14:42 York to Plymouth. As the former D1719/47128, the locomotive would again be re-numbered, this time as 47811 from August 1989. In the early 1990s it was given InterCity Swallow livery, which was followed by Great Western green after Privatisation in the late 1990s. 16 September 1988. (Mark Jamieson)

47461 *Charles Rennie Mackintosh* is at York with the 1V61 15:18 to Plymouth on 16 September 1988. Other than the push pull fitted subclass 47/7, this was the only other Class 47 to carry the Scotrail livery with the blue stripe. 47461 was withdrawn in 1991 after it was damaged in a shunting accident at Liverpool in 1990. (Mark Jamieson)

Early on a misty, drizzly morning an unidentified single Class 20 working bonnet first is passing Knottingley with an ex-GWR brake van, a small crane, and a BR brake van. (John Fox)

A view of Knottingley Depot on 1 October 1988 with Class 56 locos in at least four different liveries. Nearest the camera is 56102 in large logo blue, 56086 in Railfreight Grey, 56068 in Railfreight Grey with the red stripe, and on the right is 56097 in the latest Railfreight Coal sector livery. The cooling towers in the background are Ferrybridge Power Station.

Three Class 56 locos lined up at Knottingley Depot on 3 July 1988. They are 56086 in Railfreight Grey, 56029 in BR Blue, and 56099 in large logo blue livery. 56086 is now preserved on the Battlefield Line in BR large logo blue livery and is named *The Magistrate's Association*.

The difference in Class 56 front ends is shown with British-built 56098 on the right and Romanian-built 56014 inside the building at Knottingley Depot on 3 July 1988. After withdrawal 56098 was preserved and has operated on various heritage railways; it is now run by UK Rail Leasing and working on the main line again.

08295 is in BR blue livery with the addition of the Thornaby red stripe on the solebar, which was added to some of their Class 08 shunters. It is resting at its home depot on Sunday 1 October 1988.

08786 has the added embellishments of a light grey roof, large numbers, red coupling rods, and red solebar. Thornaby Depot, 1 October 1988.

Railfreight Grey liveried 20122 *Cleveland Potash* at Thornaby Depot 1 October 1988. Its partner is 20119 in blue; beyond are 20118 *Saltburn-by-the-Sea* and 20165 *Henry Pease* in Railfreight livery. Beyond those are six Class 37s.

Side on portrait of 20137 *Murray B. Hofmeyr* at Thornaby Depot 1 October 1988. This was one of five Class 20s based here, which were dedicated mainly to salt and potash traffic from Boulby Mine. The other locos in this working group were 20118, 20122, 20156, and 20165, which were all in Railfreight livery with the red solebar and carried names.

Railfreight liveried 20156 has its name *H.M.S. Endeavour* painted on the red solebar. James Cook sailed in HMS *Endeavour*, which was the first ship to reach the east coast of Australia in 1770. Thornaby Depot, 1 October 1988.

20118 *Saltburn-by-the-Sea* in Railfreight Grey livery at Thornaby Depot on 3 July 1988. This loco is still in the same livery and running on the main line in 2016.

Nose-to-nose and showing off their nameplates are 20118 *Saltburn-by-the-Sea* and 20137 *Murray B. Hofmeyr* at their home depot of Thornaby on 3 July 1988. Both locos carry the coloured kingfisher, which is the Thornaby Depot logo.

20172 *Redmire* and 20028 *Bedale* have both had the Thornaby treatment with red painted solebars, white kingfisher logos, and white painted cab roofs. 20172 has also been given large bodyside numbers and has its name painted on the solebar, whereas 20028 has black nameplates. There were three more blue Class 20s with red solebars; 20070, 20173 *Wensleydale,* and 20174 *Captain James Cook R.N.* The last two had their names painted on the solebar, as on 20172. 3 July 1988.

31260 in BR Blue livery is at the re-fuelling point at Thornaby Depot. On the next track is split headcode 37353 in Railfreight Grey livery with the red stripe around the base of the body. 31260 was allocated to Immingham Depot as part of the Civil Engineers fleet.

Split headcode 37353 is at Thornaby on 1 October 1988, in the attractive Railfreight Grey with red stripe livery. This loco was renumbered from 37032 in June 1988 when it was fitted with re-geared CP7 bogies; this was reversed a year later when it was returned to its original number. This loco was allocated to the Railfreight Distribution Sector at Tinsley Depot at Sheffield.

A visitor to Thornaby Depot on 1 October 1988 is 37059 in ex-works Railfreight Speedlink livery. It has been dressed up with black split headcode boxes, *Port of Tilbury* nameplates, and the Stratford depot crest featuring the Jack Sparrow. Both plates, unusually, have blue backgrounds.

During the late 1980s period, 37501 *Teesside Steelmaster* and 37502 *British Steel Teesside* were often seen together working metals trains to and from the Teesside area. 37501 was in a special British Steel blue livery adorned with large double arrows, large bodyside numbers, and a coloured kingfisher depot logo, whilst 37502 was in the more standard Railfreight Grey with red stripe livery. 37501 was renumbered to 37601 in 1995 and was taken over by DRS in 2008. (Pete Nurse)

During 1988, all the 37/5 subclass locos 37501 to 37521 were allocated to the Railfreight Metals sector at Thornaby Depot and most of them could be found at their home at weekends. On Sunday 3 July 1988 were 37518 and 37515, both in Railfreight red stripe grey livery; beyond are 37509 in Railfreight Grey and 37511 *Stockton Haulage* in the new Metals Sectorisation livery.

37504 *British Steel Corby* in Railfreight Grey livery stabled at the head of a line-up of eight Railfreight Class 37/5s at Thornaby Depot – three of which have had the red stripe added to the lower bodyside. The other locos are 37506 *British Steel Skinningrove*, 375xx, 37507, 37503 *British Steel Shelton*, 375xx, 37518, and 37514. (Pete Nurse)

47363 *Billingham Enterprise* is at its home depot of Thornaby. It has a white kingfisher depot logo on its bodyside and is in the red stripe Railfreight Grey livery. In 1994 this loco was renumbered to 47385 when it was converted for multiple working; the following year it was renumbered back to 47363 and finally scrapped in 2010. (Pete Nurse)

Another unique Thornaby livery is carried by 47361 *Wilton Endeavour*, with the yellow band along the lower bodyside plus white and orange cantrail lining. The Class 47 loco behind is 47305, which has a similar livery but without the cantrail lining. These were the only two locos to have the short-lived lower bodyside yellow stripe. (Pete Nurse)

47225 at Thornaby Depot on 1 October 1988 in standard blue livery with the added orange cantrail stripe. It started life in 1965 as D1901 before renumbering to 47225 in 1974. It was rebuilt and re-engined in 2003 as 57307 *Lady Penelope* for Virgin Trains and was later taken over by Direct Rail Services.

Three Class 47s in different liveries at Thornaby Depot on 3 July 1988. They are 47051 in standard BR Blue, 47107 in Railfreight Grey, and 47361 *Wilton Endeavour* in the new Railfreight Sectorisation livery, with the red and yellow diamond Speedlink logo. All three of them have since been scrapped – 47051 in 2000, 47107 in 1994, and 47361 in 2004.

56132 *Fina Energy* in large logo blue livery at Thornaby Depot on 1 October 1988. 56132 was subsequently painted into the Railfreight Coal sector livery, followed by Transrail livery, and was scrapped in 2006.

56124 *Blue Circle Cement* in large logo blue livery at Thornaby Depot on 1 October 1988. 56124 lost its nameplates when it was repainted into Coal Sector livery, which was later followed by Trainsrail livery. In 2006 the loco was refurbished and renumbered to 56302 for Fastline Freight and is still running today in the Colas fleet and livery.

A pair of blue Class 20s – 20008 and 20144 – heading east at South Bank with four TTA fuel oil tanks on 4 July 1988. 20008 has large bodyside numbers and has had the discs removed from the cab front, while a plate has been fitted between the cab windows. Both locos carry the Thornaby Depot coloured kingfisher logo. 4 July 1988.

Green liveried 20064 and BR blue 20092 at South Bank with empty BAA and BBA steel wagons from Lackenby steel works. 20064 and 20030 were both painted in the green livery in 1987. 4 July 1988.

20028 *Bedale* and 20172 *Redmire* with limestone wagons from Redmire Quarry to Redcar steel works at South Bank on 5 July 1988. This was a daily service that ran until the end of 1992.

20165 *Henry Pease* and 20122 *Cleveland Potash* at South Bank 4 July 1988. It is empty potash wagons heading for Boulby Mine; the wagons are bogie PFAs with one four-wheel PFA in the centre of the train and each carry two Cobra potash containers. 20165 was named after Henry Pease, who was instrumental in helping to get the railway extended to reach Saltburn, which was the making of the town. He later served as a member of Parliament.

Thornaby celebrities 20137 *Murray B. Hofmeyr* and 20118 *Saltburn-by-the Sea* in the pouring rain at South Bank with rock salt from Boulby Mine. The rock salt is carried in four-wheel open wagons and pairs of containers on bogie flat wagons. 4 July 1988.

20118 *Saltburn-by-the Sea* and 20137 *Murray B. Hofmeyr* at South Bank with empty wagons for Boulby Mine on 4 July 1988. The first three wagons are Procor Covhops for carrying Potash and the open top containers are for rock salt; the containers are on four-wheel and bogie PFA wagons.

On the following day it is again 20118 *Saltburn-by-the Sea* and 20137 *Murray B. Hofmeyr* at South Bank with empty potash wagons for Boulby Mine. This time there are five PBA bogie hopper wagons. They had the nickname of 'jolly green giants', although were not so green once they had been in service for a while. 5 July 1988.

20028 *Bedale* and 20172 *Redmire* at Thornaby station with loaded limestone from Redmire, which will be used at Redcar in the steel-making process. The British Steel PGA wagons were dedicated to this service. 5 July 1988.

31227 is turning in to the steelworks at South Bank with empty wagons on 5 July 1988. The DMU at the platform is heading for Bishop Auckland. 31227 was new as D5653 in 1960 at Finsbury Park depot; it was withdrawn late in 1988 and cut up at Vic Berry's scrapyard in Leicester the following year.

Railfreight Grey livery 31125 is heading west at Cargo Fleet with a selection of loaded steel wagons on 5 July 1988. 31125 was originally numbered D5543 when first put into traffic in 1959; it was finally withdrawn in 1994.

BR Blue 37153 is heading west with a steel train at South Bank on 5 July 1988. The BAA and BBA wagons are loaded with steel slabs. D6853 was built in 1963 and renumbered to 37153 in 1973. Within a few weeks of this photo being taken 37153 was transferred to Scotland, where it received large logo blue livery. Later, in 1991, it was repainted into the Civil Engineers grey and yellow Dutch livery.

Split headcode 37098 has a short loaded steel train with a mix of wagons and loads at South Bank 5 July 1988. This loco was later repainted into the Civil Engineers grey and yellow Dutch livery.

37516 in Red Stripe Railfreight livery has charge of a partially fitted freight at South Bank on 4 July 1988. The train has a brake van as there is very little brake force; the BDA and SPA are the only air braked wagons, the rest are MDW mineral wagons with a through air pipe. 37516 is still running today as part of the West Coast Railways Company fleet in their maroon livery.

37521 was the final 37/5 in the 37501 to 37521 batch allocated to the Railfreight Metals Sector at Thornaby Depot and was delivered in the sector livery. It is seen here arriving at South Bank with three empty BBA steel wagons on 4 July 1988. 37521 eventually received EWS livery and spent a few years with DRS. Still in that livery it made visits to preserved railways; today it is privately owned at Barrow Hill undergoing restoration.

The 15:03 Middlesbrough to Thornaby has 31282 with three Mark 1 and one Mark 2 coaches, and is standing in for a diesel multiple unit. 31282 is in Railfreight Grey livery with the added red stripe along the bodyside. Thornaby, 5 July 1988.

An InterCity liveried high speed train forming the 16:30 Kings Cross to Sunderland via Middlesbrough. It is passing Thornaby and will return after reversal at Middlesbrough. 4 July 1988.

43068 is the leading power car of the 16:30 Kings Cross to Sunderland high speed train after it has reversed at Middlesbrough. This was the only through working between Middlesbrough and Kings Cross in 1988; the Up service in the morning departed at 06:45 from Middlesbrough and the return service arrived at 19:44. Thornaby, 4 July 1988.

Departmental Route Learning unit formed of QWV TDB 977123 and QWV TDB 9777125 is seen passing Eaglescliffe on 4 July 1988. These vehicles were introduced in 1958 as Cravens Class 105 units and converted in 1982 for route learning. 977123 was formerly driving motor brake second E51286 and 977125 was driving trailer composite E56444.

A matching pair of red stripe Railfreight Grey liveried Class 31s – 31206 and 31196 – at Eaglescliffe working 6E89 Peak Forest to Tees Yard cement. Some of the PCAs would be tripped to Middlesbrough Goods Yard, others to Eastgate Cement works to be loaded, as well as some traffic for Newcastle Railway Street. 31206 has been preserved at the Rushden Station Transport Museum where it is in Civil Engineers Dutch livery. 4 July 1988.

56124 *Blue Circle Cement* in large logo blue livery at Eaglescliffe on 20 September 1989 with a loaded Merry Go Round train.

Another of Thornaby Depot's celebrity locos was 47301 in its distinctive livery of Railfreight Grey with the red stripe with white line above and large bodyside numbers. It is seen here at Stockton heading east with the 6E50 16:12 Long Eaton to Port Clarence empty 100-ton tanks on 4 July 1988. 47301 was later given the unofficial name *Centurion* after it had been transferred to Tinsley Depot. In 1995 it became a Freightliner loco and wore the triple grey livery until it was withdrawn in 2001 and eventually scrapped in 2003.

Looking smart in its BR Blue large logo livery is recently named 47434 *Pride in Huddersfield* at South Otterington with the 18:25 Newcastle to Liverpool Lime Street service on 5 July 1988. The coaches are in the attractive Trans-Pennine livery with a Mk 1 BG heading the rake of Mk 2s. Unfortunately, this loco had an early withdrawal and was scrapped in 1993.

47120 is heading south on the East Coast Main Line at South Otterington with the 6O49 16:55 Tees New Yard to Eastleigh East Yard Speedlink on 5 July 1988. The formation contains BAA steel wagons and sliding hood steel carrying wagons, which are carrying mainly steel coil for the West Midlands. Also there are five PCA cement wagons which are probably destined for Handsworth. 47120 had the name *R.A.F. Kinloss* but the plates had been removed by 1988; it was later given the unofficial name *Osprey* while working from Tinsley Depot.

BR Blue 31118 with the southbound 6L81 15:55 Haverton Hill to March Whitemoor Yard Speedlink at South Otterington on 5 July 1988. The loco is fitted with some well-weathered miniature snowploughs. Behind the loco is a VGA van, two OTA timber carrier wagons, one 100-ton bogie tank, five TTA chemical tanks, and a Cargo Wagon bogie bolster.

A pair of BR Blue split headcode Class 37s – numbers 37038 and 37047 – are heading south at South Otterington with the 4L79 18:00 Stockton to Felixstowe North Freightliner on 5 July 1988. 37038 later had its headcode boxes removed and became part of the Direct Rail Services fleet.

A well-weathered 47422 is at Darlington with the 1E69 13:25 Liverpool to Newcastle on 21 September 1990. This loco was originally D1525 and was first put into traffic in 1963. It was withdrawn from service at the end of 1991. (Mark Jamieson)

The uniquely liveried 47475 sporting Trans-Pennine livery at Newcastle waiting to depart with the 1M43 12:16 to Liverpool. This loco was first put into traffic in 1964 as D1603 and spent its first ten years allocated to Western Region depots. It was renumbered to 47475 in 1974. 21 September 1990. (Mark Jamieson)

A full shed at Sunderland on Sunday 1 October 1988; from left to right are 56111, 56116, 56131, 56129, and 08141.

56118 in large logo blue livery at Sunderland on 1 October 1988. As with some other members of this class 56118 has its number painted on the cab front above the buffer beam. This loco later received Loadhaul livery.

Split headcode 37008 in large logo blue livery at Blyth depot. Behind is refurbished 37508 in Railfreight grey livery. 37008 was later painted into Railfreight grey livery with the red stripe with the unofficial name *Hornet*. In 1991, it was badly damaged in a collision and was withdrawn. (Pete Nurse)

20046 and 20092 are working eastwards through Barnetby on 9 October 1991 with a trainload of steel slabs.

20121 with miniature snowploughs and 20190 are passing through Barnetby on 10 June 1992 with empty steel wagons. It is the Frodingham T48 Trip and is running as 6T48 from Tinsley Yard to Grimsby Brickpit Sidings with empty steel wagons for loading with imported steel.

On 8 June 1992, 20117 and 20169 are allocated to the Scunthorpe T48 trip. This trip was manned 24 hours a day and would work trains between Grimsby, Immingham, and Tinsley, moving coils and billets for British Steel – or Arvesta metals, as it later became. They are heading west through Barnetby with a trainload of steel coil from Grimsby.

Filthy 31304 and 31205 are working 6E54 Kingsbury Oil Sidings to Humber Oil Refinery at Barnetby; 31205 is in Railfreight Petroleum livery and 31304 is in Red Stripe Railfreight livery. 9 October 1991.

31233 is in Railfreight Petroleum sub-sector livery with the Immingham depot crest on the cabside. It is heading east at Barnetby with 6D96 Welton Oil Farm to Immingham East Junction 100-ton tanks on 8 June 1992. This loco was later repainted into Dutch livery and named *Severn Valley Railway*. It was withdrawn in 2002 and was sold to Fragonset Railways, and was then sold again in 2003 to Network Rail. It was re-painted into their yellow livery and put to use on Infrastructure trains where it was still being used in 2016.

31319 and 31302, both in Railfreight Petroleum sector livery, are westbound at Barnetby with oil tanks on 10 October 1991. 31319 has been fitted with miniature snowploughs. It had previously been in Railfreight grey livery with the large logo; it was later repainted into Dutch livery and was finally withdrawn from service in 1997.

Railfreight Petroleum liveried 37891 is passing through Barnetby on 10 October 1991 with a pair of PTA iron ore tippler wagons sandwiched between two barrier wagons, with a CAR brake van at the rear. 37891 was refurbished – its previous identity was 37166. The tippler wagons were returning from Doncaster works (wagon shops) where they had been for heavy repair and general overhaul. Two redundant brake vans were converted to act as a translator to connect between the rotary buckeye couplings on the tippler wagons and a standard screw coupling.

Blue large logo liveried 37116 was a bit of a celebrity loco as it still retained the skirts above its buffers and black headcode boxes. It has the unofficial painted name *Comet* and was allocated to the Railfreight Petroleum Sector at Immingham Depot. Seen not far from home at Barnetby with a short set of 100-ton oil tanks on 10 October 1991.

With a lone photographer on the platform, 37285 and 37209 enter Barnetby station with the 6D71 10:54 Lindsey to Leeds 100-ton tanks. 37285 is in the Railfreight livery without any sector logos, 37209 is in large logo blue livery and has the unofficial painted name *Phantom*. Both locos were allocated to the Railfreight Distribution Sector at Tinsley Depot. 9 October 1991.

37517 and 37504 are entering Barnetby with loaded iron ore tippler wagons from Immingham, which are destined for Scunthorpe Steelworks. 8 June 1992.

Two of Thornaby Depot's Railfreight Metals Sector Class 37 locos – 37503 *British Steel Shelton* and 37515 – approaching Barnetby station with empty iron ore tipplers, which will be refilled at Immingham with yet another load for Scunthorpe Steelworks. 10 June 1992.

47270 *Swift* is heading west at Barnetby with 6G48 Grimsby West Marsh Sidings to Tinsley Yard imported steel coil on 8 June 1992. The loco is allocated to Tinsley Depot and has one of their painted names. After privatisation, 47270 became a Freightliner loco and wore their green and yellow livery until it was withdrawn from service in 2005. It was then taken into preservation at the Nene Valley Railway and returned to BR Blue livery. It is now privately owned and based at Carnforth, where it has returned to use on the main line.

47197 in Railfreight Petroleum Sector livery westbound at Barnetby on 10 June 1992 with 6D90 Immingham East Junction to Welton Oil Sidings 100-ton tanks. After privatisation this loco was used by Freightliner; it kept the two tone grey livery but with the Freightliner red triangle logo instead of the petroleum sector logo.

47368 *Neritidae* is passing through Barnetby working 6G85 Lindsey Oil Refinery to Hunslet East Bitumen Terminal on 10 June 1992. The nameplates were removed from this loco in 1993.

47401 *Star of the East* is passing through Barnetby with 100-ton oil tanks on 9 October 1991. This was the first Class 47 entered into service in 1962, numbered D1500 – a number which it carries again on the cabside. This loco was previously named *North Eastern* whilst allocated to Gateshead Depot; it lost its name when re-allocated to Immingham earlier in 1991 where it was repainted in 1960s style two-tone green livery and then re-named. It was withdrawn from service in 1992 and is now preserved at Butterley on the Midland Railway, once again carrying the name *North Eastern*.

56081 is passing through Barnetby with the 7G02 Immingham Bulk Terminal to Scunthorpe Coal Handling Plant MGR on 10 June 1992.

Named after the famous English naturalist and geologist, 60068 *Charles Darwin* is at Barnetby with empty iron ore tippler wagons. The working is the 6K23 Santon Ore Blending Plant to Immingham Bulk Terminal on 9 October 1991. 60068 is in Railfreight Coal Sector livery; it later received EWS logo in place of the Coal Sector logo and was withdrawn from service in 2009 and stored at Toton.

60054 *Charles Babbage* is heading east at Barnetby with the 6D71 Leeds Oil Terminal to Lindsey Oil Refinery empty oil tanks on 10 October 1991. Charles Babbage was a mathematician who was involved with inventing the first mechanical computer.

60028 *John Flamsteed* in Railfreight Petroleum Sector livery is passing Barnetby with a light load of two 45-ton Bitumen tanks. It is the 6G85 Lindsey Oil Refinery to Leeds Hunslet ORT Bitumen terminal. The loco was named after John Flamsteed, who was a leading astromoner from Derbyshire where some schools and colleges carry his name. 8 June 1992.

Monday morning at Barnetby and a convoy of locos led by 31282 in Railfreight grey with the red stripe livery pass through, returning to Immingham Depot after civil engineering weekend work. Following are 31205 also in Red Stripe livery, Railfreight Grey 31184, 31276 in Railfreight Coal Sector livery, with Dutch liveried 37058 bringing up the rear. 8 June 1992.

47286 is in Railfreight livery with no sector logos but it does have the Tinsley Depot plaque on the cabside. It is working 6D36 08:10 Tees New Yard to Scunthorpe via Selby Connect Rail Trip; this conveyed steel products destined for the Continent via the Dover train ferry. The HEA in the consist is a HSA scrap wagon going to Scunthorpe to be loaded with swarf and will end up back at Lackenby with off cuts from Scunthorpe steel works. Althorpe, 9 June 1992.

47212 is working 6G85 Lindsey Oil Refinery to Leeds Neville Hill, Hunslet Depot fuel and bitumen for Neville Hill Sidings. The depot tanks would be tripped in and out by the depot pilot and the Bitumen tanks went to Hunslet East Oil Terminal. The return working saw both sets of tanks joined up at Neville Hill Sidings again. Althorpe, 9 June 1992.

Leyland Class 141, unit number 141 102, is at Althorpe on 9 June 1992. These two-car units, which have bus bodies on a four-wheel chassis, were first introduced 1984. The carriage numbers are 55502 and 55522 and they are in the red and cream livery of West Yorkshire PTE, allocated to Neville Hill, Leeds.

Refurbished heavyweight Class 37 37718 is in Railfreight Metals sector livery and fitted with miniature snowploughs. It is working 6M51 Scunthorpe BSC Entrance 'C' to Brierley Hill loaded steel working and has just crossed the River Trent on the combined road and rail King George V lifting bridge at Althorpe on 9 June 1992. The bridge was built in 1916 and was last lifted in 1956.

60003 *Christopher Wren* is working 6D71 13:35 Lindsey Oil Refinery to Leeds Hunslet Oil Terminal through Althorpe on 9 June 1992. In a 24-hour period, Lindsey Oil Refinery dispatched four trains to Leeds Hunslet Oil Terminal, each train consisting of twenty-seven tanks. A special operating instruction was issued to the signalmen at Gascoigne Wood and Peckfield to give these trains green signals all the way through the section from Hambelton to Garforth.

Railfreight Petroleum liveried 37707 and Dutch liveried 37058 at Hatfield and Stainforth station. Both the locos carry depot plaques on their cabsides; 37707 has the Eastfield Depot Scottie dog plaque and 37058 has the Immingham depot plaque. 9 June 1992.

On 8 June 1992, Railfreight Metals Sector liveried 37885 is accelerating through Scunthorpe yard with a lengthy rake of empty steel wagons, which are a mix of BAA and BDA types.

Snowplough-fitted 20121 is inside the shed at Frodingham Depot for servicing and maintenance on 8 June 1992.

Six Class 20 locos are seen at Frodingham Depot on 8 June 1992. The pair nearest the camera are 20214 and 20092; the next pair are 20094 and 20104, and in the distance are withdrawn 20042 and 20025.

The following day, 20214 has been split from its partner for a trip up the Flixborough branch. It is approaching Dragonby Exchange Sidings with loaded BDA wagons carrying steel rods from Scunthorpe Rod Mill. A privately owned shunter will collect them from the exchange sidings and take them on to Flixborough Wharf. 20214 is fitted with miniature snowploughs on the cab end only. Very few Class 20s had these fitted to the bonnet end – usually only some of those working in Scotland. 9 June 1992.

20214 is on the return trip from Dragonby Sidings and is approaching the Dawes Lane level crossing at Scunthorpe with six empty BDAs on 9 June 1992. This the 8D55/D56 trip, which was an as required working that could run up to three times a day.

Railfreight Distribution liveried 90025 with a set of Mark 4 coaches is standing in the pouring rain at Doncaster station on 8 June 1992. The Class 90 is probably standing in for a Class 91 on this Kings Cross to Newcastle service.

Class 91, believed to be 91005, approaches Colton Junction near York on the evening of 26 May 1998 with the 1N16 18:20 (FX) Kings Cross to Newcastle working. (Mark Bugler)

In the smart GNER livery High Speed Train power car 43111 with 43109 on the rear passes under Church Lane near Bolton Percy with the 1E10 07:55 Inverness to Kings Cross *Highland Chieftain*. 27 May 1996. (Mark Bugler)

A working that still runs in 2016, albeit now originating from Tees dock, is the 4L79 16:13 Wilton to Felixstowe Freightliner working. Back in the late '90s, the booked traction was a Loadhaul Class 56 loco. 56035 crosses the ladder junction onto the Church Fenton line at Colton Junction on 13 June 1996. (Mark Bugler)

The 13.79-mile Selby diversion line from Colton Junction to Temple Hirst opened in 1983 to avoid potential subsidence from the Selby coalfields. Rail Express Systems 47727 takes the East Coast Main Line at Colton Junction with the 1E24 Edinburgh to Kings Cross on 13 June 1996. Booked traction was a Rail Express Systems Class 86. By 1997 Class 325 units were in operation on this service. (Mark Bugler)

86254 takes the Selby bypass route on the ECML at Colton Junction with the 1V69 17:32 Low Fell to Bristol Temple Meads mail train. Booked traction was a RES86, which seemed strange given the destination was not electrified. 26 May 1998. (Mark Bugler)

37897 heads north at Burton Salmon with the 6E39 08:10 (MWFO) Mostyn to Hull Saltend 'Acid Tanks', whilst 59206 heads south with an unidentified National Power working with coal for one of the Aire Valley power stations. National Power introduced six Class 59/2s in 1995; in 1998 they were taken over by EWS and soon repainted into their maroon and gold livery, which has since been replaced by the DBS red livery. 27 May 1998. (Mark Bugler)

After the sale of the three main freight companies, Mainline, Transrail, and Loadhaul, to EW&S Railways, the former liveries were no longer restricted to their former areas and started to appear all over the UK. Mainline Blue liveried 60044 passes Melton Ross with 6G04 11:36 Scunthorpe to Immingham empty MGR. 1 April 1999. (Mark Bugler)

Always a working to catch because of the varied use of locos and mixed load was the 6D66 14:35 Immingham to Doncaster 'Enterprise' working. Split headcode box 37038 in Civil Engineers Dutch livery passes Melton Ross on 1 March 1999. (Mark Bugler)

One train that could always produce multiple loco moves was the 6D65 Doncaster Belmont to Immingham Enterprise. Here we see 56044 *Cardiff Canton* with 56056 and 60067 *James Clerk Maxwell*, both dead in tow on the climb from Barnetby with a very well-loaded Enterprise working. 13 September 2000. (Mark Finch)

One of the first signals to go long before the Barnetby resignalling in 2015 was here at Wrawby Junction as 56062 rumbles onto the Lincoln line passing the fine semaphore gantry with the 6v31 Immingham to Swansea MGR. 15 July 2003. (Mark Finch)

Saturday 3 March 2001 saw two Class 56 locos allocated on coal trains that were routed via the Brigg line. After waiting for the booked time here, EWS liveried 56091 *Stanton* finally gets the road working an Immingham to West Burton MGR. 56091 is still operating today with DCR and before that with Fertis. (Mark Finch)

56049 at Hatfield and Stainforth with 6D88 Goole to Scunthorpe with a curtain sided steel wagon followed by about a dozen BDA bogie bolsters which are mostly empty. 5 April 2002. (Steve Clark)

60100 *Boar of Badenoch* in EWS livery at Scunthorpe with the 6D45 Doncaster to Immingham Enterprise on 16 October 2003. The wagons are mostly Continental bogie ferry vans with a few tanks at the rear. (Steve Clark)

16 October 2003 was to be the final day of Class 56 and HAA operation on the Immingham to Scunthorpe MGR circuit. Loadhaul liveried 56106 arrives at Scunthorpe with another load of the black stuff from Immingham bulk terminal. 56106 was taken over by Fertis when withdrawn by EWS. (Mark Finch)

56094 *Eggborough Power Station* passes a fine array of semaphore signals on the approach to Gilberdyke on 2 March 2004 with 6D54 Hull to Doncaster Belmont Enterprise. The BDA bolster wagons are heading for Skinningrove and the BYAs are carrying cold reduced coils for Wolverhampton Steel Terminal. This view is now sadly gone thanks to the growth of lineside vegetation and 56094 is now in service with Colas Railfreight. (Mark Finch)

Loadhaul liveried 56083 is at Doncaster with 6D54 Hedon Road to Doncaster Belmont on 25 March 2003. The load is six BYA steel-carrying wagons. (Steve Clark)

Immingham-allocated 56102 in Loadhaul livery is approaching Doncaster on 16 May 2000 with a well-loaded 6D66 Immingham to Doncaster Belmont Enterprise. 56102 had some modifications including its engine downrated, gearing ratio and fuel diverts altered, auto sanding equipment installed – similar to the Class 60 – and modifications to its air grilles at the top. It was then involved with trials on various heavy freights in various parts of the country and although they were successful the money to do the rest of the fleet was not forthcoming as EWS from its very early days wanted to renew their locomotive fleet. (Mark Finch)

EWS liveried 56060 is passing Carlton with the 6N63 Thrislington to Steetly limestone on 6 December 2003. (Steve Clark)

56006 was a bit of a celebrity loco being in BR Blue livery in 2003; it is seen here at Cargo Fleet with the 6D78 Redcar to Scunthorpe HEA wagons loaded with coke. This train would recess in Tees Yard and depart during the afternoon. 6 December 2003. (Steve Clark)

EWS liveried 56059 is winding its way out of Tees Yard with bogie covhop potash wagons from Boulby mine. In the same livery is 08339, waiting on the right with three tank wagons. 2 April 2003. (Steve Clark)

08600 in A.V. Dawson livery is shunting three potash bogie hopper wagons at Middlesbrough goods depot on 6 December 2003. (Steve Clark)

With a backdrop of the North Sea at Hunts Cliff is 56049 with the 6F69 Middlesbrough Goods depot to Boulby mine empty potash wagons on 22 July 2003. 56049 is in the Dutch livery with the added Transrail logos. After withdrawal by EWS, 56049 was part of the Fertis fleet and is now in the process of being overhauled and eventually returned to service with Colas. (Steve Clark)

Ex-Northeast Trainload Coal 56134 *Blyth Power* drops down into Crag Hall on 3 April 2002 with a rake of PBA potash wagons destined for Boulby mine. These wagons were in the process of being phased out with the introduction of the more modern Nacco hopper wagons. (Steve Clark)

56134 *Blyth Power* is returning from Boulby with loaded potash wagons for Tees Dock at Brotton Hill on 3 April 2002. These PBA wagons were nicknamed 'jolly green giants'. (Steve Clark)

With GB Railfreight's rapidly increasing business demands, a loco shortage called for an unusual hiring to the mainline fleet. Martin Walker's 55022 *Royal Scots Grey* was called upon to work for several weeks between North Blyth and Lynemouth on the Alcan tanks. Looking and sounding great, 55022 on 6N69 leaves North Blyth with loaded wagons on 12 April 2011. (Gordon White)

With turbines of Keadby Wind Farm providing the backdrop Direct Rail Services 20302 and 20305 are approaching Althorpe in fading light with the 6Z20 16:20 York Engineering Yard to Scunthorpe Trent Yard on 8 October 2013.

66109 at Hatfield and Stainforth with five EWS 100-ton oil tanks; it is the 6D79 08:34 Lindsey to Neville Hill depot fuel oil. 9 October 2013.

Plenty of coal stock at Hatfield Main Colliery as 66069 is leaving with the 6F29 09:45 loaded coal to Cottam Power Station. The colliery first opened in 1916 and finally closed in June 2015. 9 October 2013.

Freightliner 66555 is heading north through Hatfield and Stainforth station with the 6M05 09:30 Scunthorpe Roxby to Northenden empty binliner. 9 October 2013.

66082 is heading south at Burton Salmon with the 08:38 Hull to Drax Power Station loaded biomass. The biomass pellets are shipped to the docks at Hull from Canada and the United States. 20 October 2015. (Simon Lindsell)

East Coast Class 91 91113 is slowing for the Doncaster stop with the 1S10 10:00 Peterborough to Edinburgh. On this day not all services were running to and from Kings Cross. 18 April 2014.

The 1S20 14:00 Kings Cross to Aberdeen is approaching Doncaster on 18 April 2014. It is formed of an East Coast High Speed train set with power car 43257 leading and 43312 bringing up the rear.

A High Speed Train in the distinctive livery of Grand Central is forming the 1N93 12:44 London Kings Cross to Sunderland as it speeds through Doncaster on 18 April 2014. The leading power car is refurbished 43457, which is also fitted with buffers.

GBRF 66735 is crossing from the up through to the down through line at Doncaster station with the 4D21 14:35 Eggborough Power Station to Doncaster Down Decoy. 18 April 2014.

60059 *Swinden Dalesman* is departing from Eggborough Power Station with 6D42 13:42 empty fuel oil tanks to Lindsey Oil Refinery. Loadhaul was the previous livery for this loco. 20 October 2015.

Autumn colours are beginning to show on the trees at Whitley Bridge as 66744 *Crossrail* passes the junction for Eggborough Power Station with the 4D82 13:15 Drax Power Station to Doncaster Down Decoy empty coal hoppers. 20 October 2015. (Simon Lindsell)

Power car 43316 is heading the 1E15 09:52 Aberdeen to Kings Cross High Speed Train at Burn on 20 October 2015. This set is in the latest Virgin livery for these High Speed Trains on the East Coast route. Behind the power car are two first class coaches followed by a buffet car and six standard class coaches, with the second power car at the rear.

91127 is speeding north with the 1N21 14:30 Kings Cross to Newcastle at Burn on 20 October 2015. The loco is still in the East Coast silver livery with the rake of Mk 4 coaches in the new Virgin livery for this route.

The 1E44 11:46 Southampton to Newcastle is passing Burn formed of an Arriva Cross Country four-car class 220 Voyager unit. These units were first introduced in 2000 by Virgin Trains. The cooling towers and chimney of the Drax Power Station can be seen on the horizon. 20 October 2015.

EWS 66016 has just left the Lackenby Steelworks with the 6D11 13:23 departure to Scunthorpe Steelworks. The location is South Bank station. Disappearing into the distance is the 12:53 Darlington to Saltburn formed of Pacer unit 142 015. 21 October 2015.

66414 in the latest Class 66 Freightliner livery is rounding the curve at Cargo Fleet with the 4L79 15:55 Tees Dock to Felixstowe containers. 66414 was previously part of the DRS fleet before transferring to Freightliner. 21 October 2015.

66571 is at South Bank with the 4D07 14:48 Tees Dock to Leeds Freightliner on 21 October 2015. During 2015 there were two daily Freightliner workings from Tees Dock – this one and 4L79 to Felixstowe.

66546 is entering the branch to Tees Dock at Grangetown with the 6F32 09:34 from Boulby Mine with NACCO hopper wagons loaded with potash. It is about to cross a minor road crossing, which still has a picture of a steam engine on the warning sign. 22 October 2015.

On 28 June 2016, Freightliner Class 66 66531 is at Middlesbrough Goods with a rake of NACCO bogie hopper wagons, which will be returning to Boulby Mine for re-loading. (Simon Lindsell)

Pacer unit 142 092 is forming the 2D42 13:25 Bishops Auckland to Saltburn as it passes Redcar Steel Works. 22 October 2015.

A contrast in scenery for 66546 with the backdrop of Redcar Steelworks and Coatham Marsh nature reserve on the other side of the track. The train is the 6F31 07:10 Tees Dock to Boulby mine empty potash hoppers. 22 October 2015. (Simon Lindsell)

In 2013 GBRF repainted two of their Class 66 locos with special liveries for the 150th anniversary of the London Underground. 66718 was named *Sir Peter Hendy CBE*, who was the Transport for London commissioner. On 18 November 2015, 66718 is seen heading the 4R62 11:20 Doncaster Down Decoy to Immingham empty coal hoppers at Worlaby Carrs.

TATA Steel liveried 60099 is at Worlaby Carrs with 6K25 15:17 Santon to Immingham empty iron ore tipplers. 18 November 2015.

First TransPennine Express unit 185 113 is crossing Worlaby Carrs on 18 November 2015 – it is the 1B81 13:26 Cleethorpes to Manchester Airport. 151 of these air-conditioned three-car units are in service with TransPennine; each car is powered by a 750 hp diesel, giving the unit a total of 2,250 hp.

Colas Rail Freight liveried 60056 is at Worlaby Carrs with the 12:04 West Holmes Junction to Lindsey Refinery empty tanks. Colas acquired ten Class 60s from DB Schenker in 2014; they were overhauled at Toton Depot. 18 November 2015.

66165 is travelling around the freight-only curve from Ulceby to Brocklesby with the 17:01 Immingham to Santon loaded iron ore tippler wagons. 19 April 2014.

Passing the Singleton Birch Lime Works at Melton Ross in glorious weather on 12 March 2014 is 60024 hauling 6T24 11:41 Immingham to Santon Ore Terminal, which is at Scunthorpe Steel Works. (Mark Jamieson)

66164 is hauling 1M00 11:40 Humber Oil Refinery to Kingsbury past the Singleton Birch Lime Works at Melton Ross. 12 March 2014. (Mark Jamieson)

Direct Rail Services 20302 and 20303 top and tail the railhead treatment train and are captured here passing the infamous lime works at New Barnetby, forming the 3S14 Grimsby to Bridlington. 9 October 2015. (Mark Bugler)

60040 *The Territorial Army Centenary* has a very light load with the 6V19 17:22 Immingham to Llanwern at Melton Ross on 17 April 2014. The wagons are a BAA loaded with steel coil and a curtain sided steel wagon

66531 and hoppers in Freightliner livery forming the 4R14 11:30 Ratcliffe Power Station to Immingham empty coal hoppers at Melton Ross on 8 October 2013.

Seen heading through Knabbs Crossing, between Barnetby and Melton Ross, is GBRf's foreign import 66750. It is seen working the Doncaster Down Decoy to Immingham HIT empty coal hoppers on 17 April 2014. It arrived in this country from Germany in June 2013 and entered service the following December. It was repainted into GBRF's house colours in 2015 and now carries the name *Bristol Panel Signal Box*. (Andy Picton)

Colas Rail Freight 60021 has charge of the 6E32 08:55 Preston Docks to Lindsey Oil Refinery made up of eight empty bogie bitumen tanks – a light load for a Class 60. Knabbs Bridge, 19 October 2015.

Considering how industrial surrounding areas are such as Scunthorpe, Immingham, and Grimsby are, North Lincolnshire is also an attractive, and quite rural area. Just a stone's throw away from all this heavy industry, 185 118 passes Knabbs Bridge on the approach to Barnetby working 1B79 12:26 Cleethorpes to Manchester Airport. 12 March 2014. (Mark Jamieson)

Knabbs Hill just east of Barnetby provides the viewpoint for EWS 66109 as it accelerates away from the station with the 4C72 09:42 Scunthorpe to Immingham empty coal hoppers. 8 October 2013.

60066 was repainted into the Drax 'Powering Tomorrow' silver livery after overhaul at Toton in 2013; it was to mark the beginning of Biomass trains to Drax Power Station. It is seen here at Barnetby on 17 November 2015 with the 6M00 14:30 Humber Refinery to Kingsbury tanks.

66747 is in GBRF grey livery at Barnetby with the 6F59 14:45 Immingham to Cottam Power Station loaded coal hoppers on 17 November 2015. This loco was imported from Holland with sister locos 66748 and 66749 in December 2012. All three of them entered service during the summer of 2013 in grey livery; they were all repainted into GBRF's standard livery during 2016 at Eastleigh's Arlington Works.

GBRF's 66721 *Harry Beck* is second GBRF loco to be repainted in a unique livery for the 150th anniversary of the London Underground. It is painted white with different Tube maps on either side – one being the 2013 map and the other from 1933. It is passing Barnetby with the 6C09 08:45 Immingham to Eggborough Power Station loaded coal hoppers. 19 October 2015.

EWS liveried 66213 at Barnetby on 18 April 2014 with the 6C79 16:41 Immingham Bulk Terminal to Scunthorpe BSC loaded coal hoppers. Freightliner locos are now hauling these coal trains and also the associated iron ore services, which they took over in 2016.

60015 in DB Schenker red livery is passing Barnetby East signal box with the 6M24 17:13 Lindsey Oil Refinery to Kingsbury 100-ton tanks. 18 April 2014.

Tata Steel liveried 60099 is approaching Barnetby East Signal Box with the 6T22 08:02 Immingham to Santon loaded iron ore for Scunthorpe Steel Works. 17 November 2015.

Later the same day, 60099 is passing the soon-to-be-closed Wraby Junction Signal Box with the 6T24 11:38 Immingham to Santon loaded iron ore tipplers. 17 November 2015.

Freightliner's 66519 approaching Barnetby station with the 09:33 Barrow Hill to Immingham empty coal hoppers. 19 October 2015.

One of the last Class 60s still running in EWS livery in 2015 was 60065 *Spirit of Jaguar*. It is seen here approaching Barnetby with the 6E46 04:37 Kingsbury to Lindsey empty tanks. These heavy oil trains run twice a day from Humberside to Birmingham and are normally hauled by Class 60 locos. 23 October 2015.

66084 is passing through Barnetby with the 6D13 17:39 Drax Power Station to Lindsey Oil Refinery empty fuel oil tanks. 66522 in its special one-off Shanks Freightliner livery is in the yard with the 17:27 Doncaster to Immingham empty coal hoppers. 66522 is about to be refuelled from a road tanker. 17 April 2014.

As dusk approaches 60011 is heading towards Barnetby with the 6E41 11:35 Westerleigh to Lindsey tanks; on the right is the 16:35 Doncaster to Immingham empty coal hoppers. 19 October 2015.

Bibliography

Ian Allan abc, *British Rail: Motive Power Combined Volume* (Various years)

Platform 5 Publishing Ltd, *British Railways Locomotives and Coaching Stock* (Various years)

Rail Express Magazine

Rail Magazine

www.Class47.co.uk